Frances H

Snow Light, Water Light

with drawings by Paul Stangroom

BLOODAXE BOOKS

ISBN: 0 906427 69 X

First published 1983 by
Bloodaxe Books Ltd,
P.O. Box 1SN,
Newcastle upon Tyne NE99 1SN.

Second impression 1984

Bloodaxe Books Ltd acknowledges
the financial assistance of Northern Arts.

ACKNOWLEDGEMENTS

Thanks are due to the editors of *Argo, Arts North, New Poetry 8* (Arts Council—P.E.N./Hutchinson, 1982), *Poetry Now* (BBC Radio 3), *PN Review, Poetry Review* and *Writing Women*, where these poems were first published or broadcast.

'January' first appeared in *A Garland of Poems for Leonard Clark on his 75th Birthday* (Enitharmon Press, 1980).

Four of these poems first appeared, with Paul Stangroom's drawings, in *Wall* (LYC Gallery, 1981).

Six of these poems appeared in *Presences of Nature* (Carlisle Museum & Art Gallery, 1982).

Particular thanks are due to Northern Arts whose provision of a Writer's Award furnished the time in which these poems were written.

Printed in Great Britain by
Tyneside Free Press Workshop Ltd, Newcastle upon Tyne.

For Roger and Adam
who shared the farmhouse

January

A sealed stillness
– only the stream moves,
tremor and furl of water
under dead leaves.

In silence
the wood declares itself:
angles and arabesques of darkness,
branch, bramble,
tussocks of ghost grass
– under my heel
ice shivers
frail blue as sky
between the runes of trees.

Far up
rooks, crows
flail home.

Rain – Birdoswald

I stand under a leafless tree
more still, in this mouse-pattering
thrum of rain,
than cattle shifting in the field.
It is more dark than light.
A Chinese painter's brush of deepening grey
moves in a subtle tide.

The beasts are darker islands now.
Wet-stained and silvered by the rain
they suffer night,
marooned as still as stone or tree.
We sense each other's quiet.

Almost, death could come
inevitable, unstrange
as is this dusk and rain,
and I should be no more
myself, than raindrops
glimmering in last light
on black ash buds

or night beasts in a winter field.

Poem found at Chesters Museum, Hadrian's Wall

To Jove, best and greatest
and to the other immortal gods;
to Augustus, happy and unconquered
Victory, holding a palm branch;
to Hadrian
commemorating 343 paces of the Roman Wall

bill hook, holdfast, trivet
latch lifter, nail lifter, snaffle bit
sickle blade, terret ring, spear butt
boat hook, entrenching tool
chisel, gouge, gimlet, punch

To Longinus, trumpeter
and Milenus, standard bearer
1st Cohort of the Batavians;
to Cornelius Victor
served in the army 26 years
lived 55 years 11 days
erected by his wife;
to Brigomaglos, a Christian;
to my wife Aelia Comindus
who died aged 32

unguentaria
balsamaria
ivory comb
pins of bronze and bone
dress fastener
strap fastener
spinning whorls
needles, spoons
Millefiori beads
ligula, earprobe
tongs

To the woodland god Cocidius;
to Coventina, water goddess
and attendant nymphs

– in her well
axe hammer
spiral ring, jet ring
dogbrooch, coins

To the Mother Goddesses
to the gods of this place
to the goddesses across the water
to the old gods
to a god...

dedication partly obliterated
with human figure in rude relief
text of doubtful meaning
dedication illegible

uninscribed

stone of...

The Crooked Glen

I saw nothing but waves and winds

...the moon resting in a broken apple tree
an ushering wind shake ash and alder
by the puckered river.
Lightly, like boats, the thin leaves rock and spin.

Blood-dark berries stir; above my head the thorn trees
lean.
In their black pools the moon fragments herself.

Ghost dry the unquiet reeds...

I saw nothing but the waters wap
and waves wan

Camboglanna or the Crooked Glen is one
of the reputed sites of Arthur's last battle.

Brigomaglos, a Christian, speaks...

'Some say they saw the Bull,
stamping under the skyline
with the new sun rising between his horns.
They say the black blood flows like water...

I don't believe them.
It was only the officers,
never the men
(any god would do for us
till the White Christ came).
They'd see anything, anyway,
stumbling out of their caves
dizzy with darkness and the stink of blood.

Strange how they thought they brought the light to birth.

We pulled their temple down in the end,
opened it up to the proper light
– plenty of black birds flapping around
but never their Raven that flies to the sun.

We have the Sun,
our Christ is the Son who is brought to birth.
He is a white Dove
who walks in fields of light,
brighter than snow-light or water-light.
His light burns in us.
He has engraved our souls like glass
to hold his seeds of light.

Those old gods should keep their place
under the dark of stones
or in the deep wood.
They should fade like the last wood-ember
or the last sputtering flame of the lamp,
be echoed only in children's songs.

In sleep they crowd
riding the uneasy edge of dreams...'

The Mithraic Temple at Carrawburgh is believed to have been pulled down by Christians in A.D. 297.

Stone

iron-culled
obdurate harvest

endures our purpose
without blood or cry

sundered, hewn
can stone give comfort to stone?

outlasts flame, petal, bone

is the sleep of stars

will ripen to its own season

Irthing Valley

a field of stones
a river of stones

each stone in its place

can a star be lost
or a stone?

uncountable
the constellations of stone

the wind lays itself down
at dusk
a fine cloth over the stones

the river is dispossessed
it casts up white branches
roots
shoals of white sand

it cannot oust its stones

between air and water
my shadow
laving the stones

Sightings

Flake on flake, snow
packed light as ash
or feather,
shavings of crystal.
By moonlight
stars pulse underfoot.

The burning fox ran here,
his narrow print
under gate
and over wall
diagonal across the field;
skeining of rabbit tracks,
our own slurred trail.

Like black stones
crows squat, sunning
among staring sheep
– crow's wing
brushed on snow,
three strokes
twice etched
as faint and fine
as fossil bone.

Flowers

(for Winifred Nicholson)

Flowers,
a dozen or more,
I picked one summer afternoon
from field and hedgerow.
Resting against a wall
I held them up
to hide the sun.
Cell by cell,
exact as dance,
I saw the colour,
structure, purpose
of each flower.
I named them with their secret names.
They flamed in air.

But, waking
I remember only two
– soapwort and figwort,
the lilac and the brown.
The rest I guess at
but cannot see
– only myself,
almost a ghost upon the road,
without accoutrement,
holding the flowers
as torch and talisman
against the coming dark.

For Stephen Procter
on seeing his exhibition of forms in glass

Perfected whiteness
– a stellar littoral, bright
beyond bone or pearl.

Spiral chambers sing of
sea's breath, the curve
and fall of flowers.

Cave within a cave
of quiet, thought becomes music;
litanies of light resolve

in gathering trance.
A whorl of shadow
trembles, brims.

Oh wave and silence,
breaking still
in shining arcs of air.

Vindolanda – January

  winter light
a track through trees
leaning with frozen snow;
boy and dogs whoop ahead,
in a white flurry
vanish over the near horizon

  slush, mud underfoot
the sign-post obscured

  Vindolanda
a word warm on the tongue
– voices returning
bronze glint by firelight
smoke from the hill

  over the black burn
through stark trees
a stone tower
  white shrouded,
blue shadowed humps in the land

  birds hop, silent
a moon sharpens the yellow sky

  snow drives into the angled field

  on the map of the land
boy, dogs wheel and turn
perspectives away

Finding a Sheep's Skull

Sudden shock of bone
at the path's edge,
like a larger mushroom
almost hidden by leaves.

I handle the skull gently
shaking out earth and spiders.
Loose teeth chock in the jaw:
it smells of nothing.

I hold it up to sunlight,
a grey-green translucent shell.
Light pours in
like water
through blades and wafers of bone.
In secret caves
filaments of skull hang down;
frost and rain have worked
to shredded lace.

The seasons waste its symmetry.
It is a cathedral
echoing spring; in its decay
plainsong of lamb
and field and sun
inhabits bone.

The shallow cranium
fits in my palm

– for speculative children
I bring it home.